Accolades for Lorcán Black

Lorcán Black leads you on a trek to the middle of the forest, where all the magick and ghosts lie, and then to the ward where the reality is. *Rituals* can speak to all of us, it emits from within, the "same mad frequency" that allures us. The language of the occult is a familiar one that Black reiterates with subtle grace, reminiscent of Frost and Plath. However, we must remember how we got here, what are we to do now that we are here, trapped and reflecting of our own woes. "There are four walls, a window, an exit. / And that thing trapped inside / could be an animal." *Rituals* is a stunning debut that I wish to never emerge from."
- Josh Dale, owner of Thirty West Publishing House

I see the poems in Lorcán Black's *Rituals* as seeking poems. They seek clarity, justice, and sanity in a world that offers too little of these things. Black's poems reckon with the past, with religion, with country, and with the mind—"despair…a lesson in needlework / a black-stitched pattern." What I found in *Rituals* is an attentiveness to image that feels like conjuring, and an excavation of beauty from darkness: "diamonds / in the bowels of a cavern."
- Maggie Smith, author of *The Well Speaks of Its Own Poison*

A beautiful collection—utterly profound and deep. I shall surely be returning to it.
- Nayankika Saikia, *Pretty Little Bibliophile*

"Fortunately, [Black] can reach our souls with a touch of delicate words frozen on ice, hot as fire, that take of all of our masks. Cuts deep into the scars, physical and metaphorical."
- João Pinho, *STYLE Magazine*

"Pale stars wink jealousies at my feet and I walk godly." Lorcán Black's *Rituals* is the restless, roaming lovechild of Neruda and Trakl, with some fiery genetic material borrowed from Plath, as well. These poems walk toward and through wreckage at once ordinary and surreal–a family, an asylum, a body learning fraught desires, the "eerie / whiteness" of Antarctica, and a "window suck[ing] its slice of moon / in the mirror of its mouth." Piercing in its vulnerability, this book often achieves a magical authority at the same time. Black dares to speak in the voice of a sorcerer, an oracle, a god: "Watch: I shall call the elements, / I shall cast sacrilegious circles in sand." This is a collection of dark yet gleaming marvels.
- Chen Chen, author of *When I Grow Up I Want to Be a List of Further Possibilities*

Reading *Rituals,* I am struck, again and again, by the power of music and imagery. When Lorcán Black writes, "a sea of poppies bloom in me," and "two heads loom...loving and empty, / two balloons," and "your face bathed in Paris lights...I have traced your holidays / night by night," I am reminded how the lyric poem can both convey and transcend the profound burdens of illness and desire.
- Blas Falconer, author of *Forgive the Body This Failure,* poetry editor for the *Los Angeles Review*

This isn't the run of the mill poetry collection, witchy, ritualistic, utterly enjoyable.
- Vani Armstrong, Goodreads Top Reviewer

Rituals by Lorcán Black is an arrangement of vivid images and edgy, emotional writing that also grips the reader.
- Jason DeHart, *Dr. J Reads*

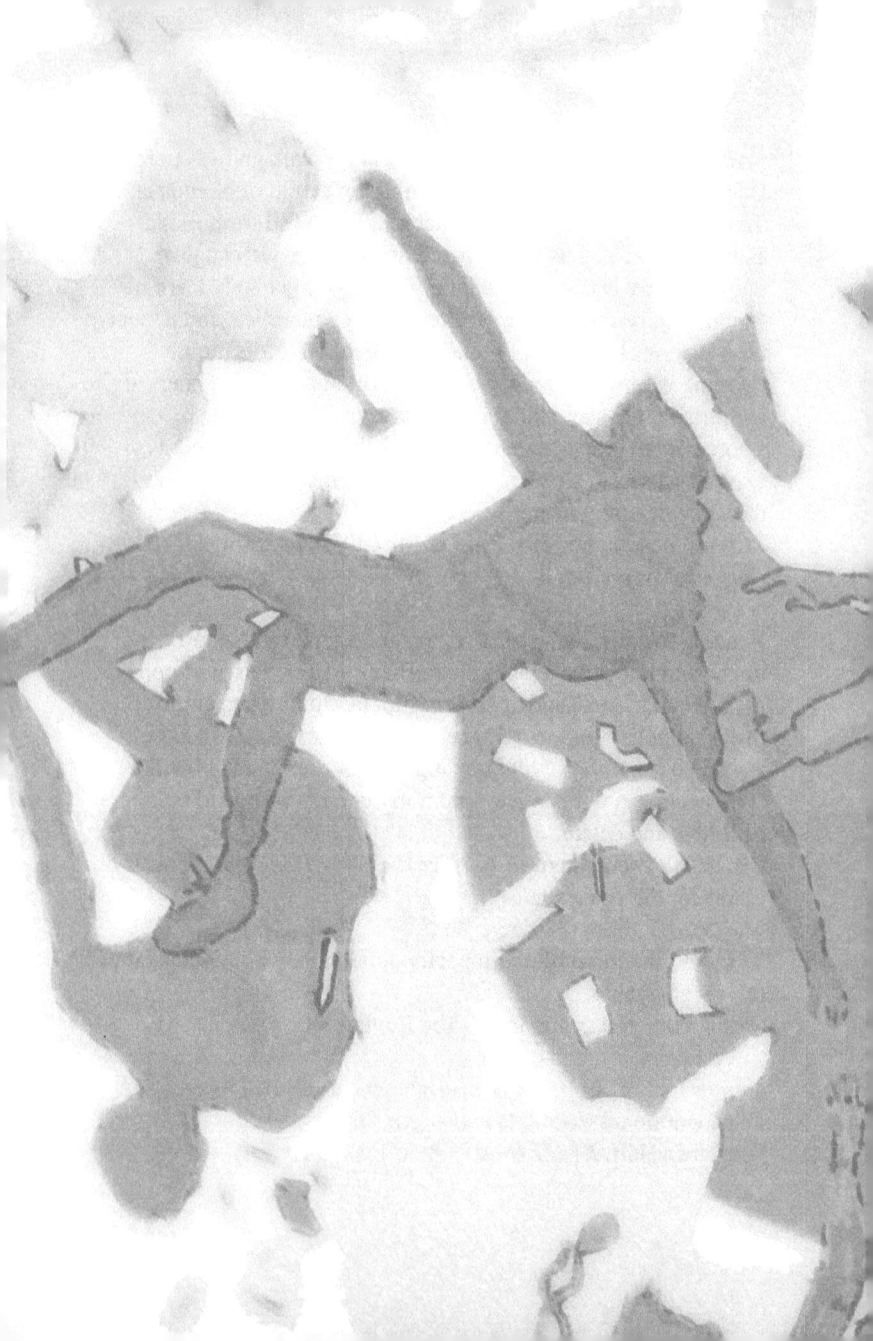

RITUALS
LORCAN BLACK
TIM DURHAM

APRIL GLOAMING

© 2019 by Lorcán Black
Illustrations © 2019 by Tim Durham

-First Edition

All rights reserved. No part of this publication may be reproduced or transmitted in any form or by any means, electronic or mechanical, including photocopy, recording, or any information storage and retrieval system, without permission in writing from the publisher.

Publisher's Cataloging-in-Publication Data

Black, Lorcán.
    Rituals / written by Lorcán Black / illustrated by Tim Durham
ISBN: 978-0-9882061-7-5

1. Poetry: General 2. Poetry: American - General I. Title
II. Author III. Illustrator

Library of Congress Control Number: 2019936671

edited by:

J. Joseph Kane,
Matt Johnstone,
& Lance Umenhofer

Art Edited by:
Robyn Leigh Lear

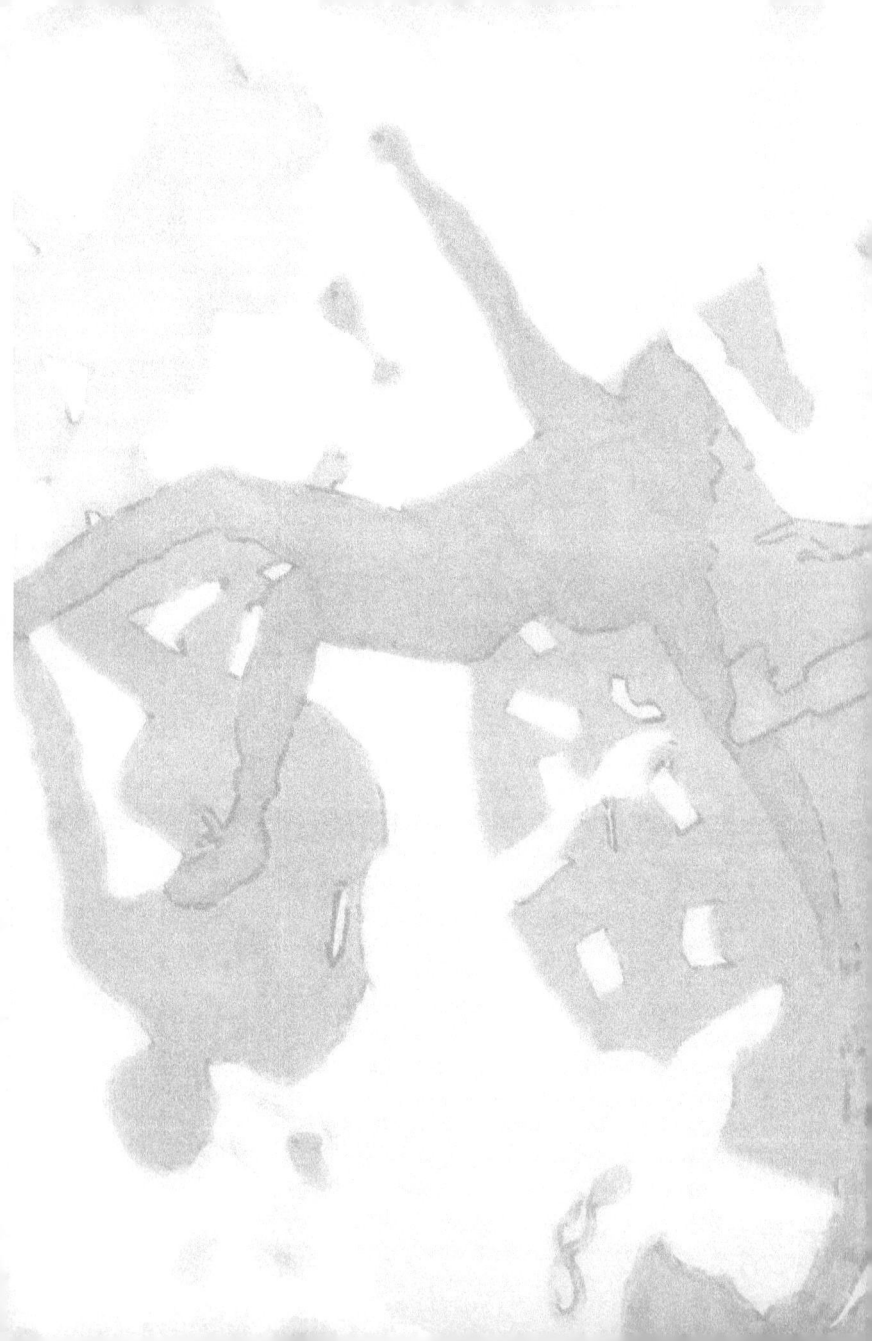

Dedicated with great love
to all my family & friends.

CONTENTS

Invocation of Ishtar	13
Magdalene Laundry	18
Ritual	21
The Gorse Fire	23
Tapestry	25
Asylum	29
Trifling Details of Great Importance	32
The Convalescent	34
The Snare	37
The Trapper's Monologue	40
A Lesson in Needlework	43
And threads that are golden don't break easily	45
Kotel	48
The Final Time I Spoke to Ruth	50
Aleppo	52
White Nights in St. Petersburg	54
Fields	58

Witness	60
Howth	64
What the Light Does to Us	68
Meteorites	71
Teddy	72
The Émigré	74
How to Bake a Marital Desertion	77
"I am always like Venice..."	79
Rainstorm	81
Hypochondria	82
Domesticity	84
Antarctica	86
Ghost in the Machine	91
The Hike	93
Nightwatch	94
For O.	96
Acknowledgements	98

Invocation of Ishtar

The moon is no mother.
Like her, you are cold and impassive

and unmoved by anything.

Bitter womb,
expelling its five ineradicable
fruits.

You might have been a Nefertiti,
a white Ishtar
bewitching your inexhaustible line of men
one after another,

a trail of bawling
offspring glittering your wake.

I could try to put you together,
broken idol
whose pieces do not fit.

But it is futile.
It is a fetish of wax.
I shall never have the whole of you.

I have only what I can piece together.
It is not much, but it will do.

Rituals

These are my ingredients:

it begins and ends
with metal on concrete–
a smattering of blood and glass,
a shadow, a whisper;

something about your fiancé
and a fatality.

As though something in you
found the fatal thread
and cut and cut
and cut–

unalterable.

In your honour, Mother,
I too have harvested the hearts of men.

Lovingly, I have lined their hearts
in canopic jars about my bed.

At night they bleed and bloom
brilliant as night flowers.

Their ghosts keep me company.

Their blood scent spumes
sweeter than all the incense of Assyria.

To them, I resemble a kind of god:
Marble-hearted and coldly unknowable,

I am the tree of knowledge
unloosing its fruit
for mouths too feeble to eat it

before the flickering tongue
of the serpent, twisted in its limbs.

Truth is a thing of beauty, it hisses,
uncoiling its gift of fruit.

Those nights in bars,
all the white-hot fits of soaring highs
and then the inevitable
plummet–

the voices, the crying in the night
to your sister,
your psychiatrist,
yourself;

every witch doctor who oversaw
every random pregnancy

and you,
who stared at the glassed-off face of oblivion
and picked up a straw.

Rituals

There were seven of us in that fatality:
You and Him

and the five of us.

Years later,
shot up with electricity
like the national grid
bottles of untouched pills for familiars,
stewed in alcohol

I came along.

Like a radio-wave
I picked up the same mad frequency.

Nine months I pickled
and like a full-blown witch
I invoked all your elation and despair.

I invoked two people,
two elements:

Light and dark.

Lorcán Black

I am insatiable,
and ache by some melancholy
that lashes me on indefatigable,
toward some dark address.

You the black shore I have broken away from,
madness a simple tithe.

Blackness foams my oars.
Watch: I shall call the elements,

I shall cast sacrilegious circles in sand.

We are inseparable, you and I.

At birth I stole your face,
I stole your volatility–
your lust that agonises and cries
before the face of its own depravity.

Unmoored,
and desolate as a heart,
bleak as the fate of Ishtar.

Magdalene Laundry

"Their lives were fleeting, but they were real and they deserve acknowledgement." – Journalist Jennifer O'Connell, on the fate of the Tuam Babies.

Name your sins in Our Fathers and Hail Marys.
Repeat them as you work–
the dishes do not do themselves.
The Sisters say,
>*'You cannot be cleansed so easily.'*

They say,
>*'God is not so merciful as to be blind.'*

There are naked girls lined up in the courtyard.
They are filth. They have sinned.
It doesn't matter what for.

Ignore them, you have no choice.
They are nothing. They are trees.
Their bare breasts just apples.
Their children merely fruit that have fallen.

All night they have been howling out, impetuous–
you hear the nuns say,
>*'You were never fit to be mothers.'*

They say,
>*'The Lord, in His infinite mercy, folded them back into–'*

a dark mouth of bones in a field of long grass–
the stench and silence of a mass grave
no better than a drum.

Shut the window. Keep scrubbing.
Do not listen, do not look–
it is only the wind that whistles
and flagellates the stones.

                'Do not concern yourself with whores.'

The Sister says,

                'In a couple weeks, you'll forget.'

But what does she know?
Her blank face pink like the slapped arse of a baby
crying its birth-fright.

She knows nothing of nights
when the weight and roar of despair
will descend from the ceiling
and drop

down to the last dregs of the bottle,
the drunk void an illusion
revealing beyond its bruised crease

a glint of false promises
just out of reach–

                diamonds
                in the bowels of a cavern.

Rituals

You, at least, will be let go.
When the day comes, the gate opens
and slams on a street, a bus stop–
an empty belly with nothing to show for it.

Over the walls there is wailing– you hear it:
the short smart smack of ash sticks on backs.
And the long grass whispering over the bones.

And all your children given,
and scattered like geese.

This is freedom now,
and the weight of it like a sentence–
shoved out from the convent to an empty street.

There is no rowing back.

For the love of God,
just forgive yourself.
Just live with it.

                    Release.

Ritual

Somewhere above an intercom crackles and buzzes–
the voice of God?

And these other bodies down here–
stupid and graceless,
vile in their proximities
in the dust and hot air.

Trains slam out of tunnels,
erupting and fleeting–
great, mechanical shafts
shunting out the hours.

Warm carriages envelop me
with their waves of light.
They feel like home.

This is the essence of love:
hands against the glass,
vacuum–packed against some foreign chest
and this strangled immediacy;
strangers sharing a breath.

For an instant
our eyes mirror one another like lovers.
One blink and the thread dissolves,
the doors slice open–

Ceremonial.

The Gorse Fire

The moon is astonishing the sky.
The mother of all pearl,
bald in her white gleam,

and the virginal purity of it–
incredulous and bright as an eye
over the fires that burn in the furze.

The stark gold spikes of the gorse
shrivel like heretics, they burn in a purge–
their hot petals ascending in soot.

See?
This is our evidence–
they are guilty, their branches–
how they crackle and snap.

Smoke strangles the wilderness,
rolling its carpets of carbon monoxide.

Rituals

In the Hollow, the foxes are crying–
each cough bled down to a hacked bark.

The bushes are lethal as faggots,
the fires are ringing them in
so that I can't bear to look at them.

Their vague, stricken shapes
scurrying in a mass,
frantic about the black centre,

the centre of the end
in a halo of flame.

On the wind sparks and ash rise
in a flurry, brilliant and effortless.

Smoke rolls down the slopes.
Sirens blare in the distance.

The foxes huddle and are still.

The Hollow smokes and blackens,
and the skulk drops into silence.

The moon sees this.

She too is stricken, look–
she has covered her face in ash.

Tapestry

    I.

At night I dream of a window
through which there stands a bald tree,
many aching limbs scratch the sky.

The heavens hear no prayers.
And as I walk, I drag a blackness in my wake.
The night birds know no lullabies.
How the bald head of the moon laughs cruelly at this.

The roads know no secrets or lies.

They know nothing but truths
which unfurl out ahead, great cobbled
tongues

rolling off to a destination
uncertain and unknown,
intimating nothing.

Rituals

II.

From where I am laid down
I have two views:

One is the cold metallic eye of a square mirror,
busying itself with memorising the opposite wall;
and a window, swallowing and releasing a single moth.

The moth is trying to bring the light with it,
crossing and re-crossing
between a light bulb and the window
and soon gives up.

This is how they shall find me, finally:
The blood-jet flooding the hot waters,
having swallowed too many pills for my penances.

All this water cleanses like a mini-Jordan.
Soon I will be whitened and pure as Christ.

III.

My ceiling now is white
with one grey smear surrounding
my naked light bulb.

I lie quite still, laid out as if for burial
as if I were King Tut.

Endless streams of gaggling heads
appear in my view with their doctoring squints.

This is a ritual.
Bind together the feathers, gather the blood in a bowl.
Smear your face in ash, smoke sage over a pyre,
burn the lanterns down low.

Watch how the silence,
like distance, enlarges itself upon me:

a shadow on a wall, relentless.

Rituals

IV.

Outside the moon tears open
like a bright hole in black cloth.

Pale stars wink jealousies at my feet and I walk godly.
The doctors chatter and glitter me with smiles.

Now I lie quite still,
clear and sharp as a pane of glass
while from the window unobtainable
stars glimmer viciously.

The statues of saints
I have adorned have all turned black.

The papers are finalised,
by morning the doctors shall set me free.

Starlight runs down my walls with the hours;
this painstaking fall into dawn.

Asylum

Definition: *(Oxford English Dictionary)*
...1.1: Shelter or protection from danger.
2. **dated** *An institution for the care of people who are mentally ill.*

In the courtyard
the manic woman is screaming.

Her walking stick at war
with the blood-red heads
of the roses.

A nurse stands idly by.
She takes notes.

I was in one piece once
until my mind bent
and broke like a river.

My last oar nothing more
than a bottle of pills
and a penance.

God is a deaf woman half gone,
knitting her gaudy silks,
each stitch a vicious mistake.

Now this: four walls
and a rubber mattress, some lunatics
and a mind twisting and untwisting
a vivid tapestry of breaks.

Rituals

Elegantly they click one
to the other, like squalid dominoes.

The doctor is an idiot;
plying me with pills that do nothing
but make me quiet and fat–

dull-eyed
and dumb as a zoo animal.

None of us know what to say.
We blink at each other as we pass,
flaming satellites in some fucked vacuum.

Let us be done with it:
let us speak of it no more
and let it off,

never again to be spoken of–
like a bad relative.

On comes the night
wielding its train of atrocities.
The stars align in perpetual bliss.

A schizophrenic has taken to calling me
Eleanor.

I am shimmering.

One white, three yellow, one blue:
one for mania, three for depression,
one for everything in succession.

Outside, my parents have parked the car.

Over the linoleum
and the stench of bleach,
their two sweet heads

loom toward me
determined,
loving and empty,

two balloons.

Trifling Details of Great Importance

The nurses eye me suspiciously if I reach for a knife
or a fork. They check I have taken my pills.

The sun rises and sets routinely.
It too checks I'm still breathing.

The leaves covertly change their colours,
so that I don't even know them.

The pills hide themselves, discretely, on the soft
wet underside of my tongue to be spat out when no–one's watching.

My parents are blank-faced, their mouths
silent and twitching.

Outside the window, a magpie
is fussing in the lower reaches of a tree.

We pretend
to be preoccupied with the scene.

In the hallway someone is screaming.
We smile at each other, politely.

Silence infiltrates each breath,
consumes our minutes.

The walls are a gentle magnolia. They do not bother us.
My mother studies them: they are of great import.

Outside, on the branches,
the berries are very still.

Like us, they seem to be waiting, asking *How?*
How did we get here?

Outside the window, a magpie
grasps something in its beak.

Wordlessly, my mother leans forward.
Watches

the blue–black wings toss air.
It is significant. Inexplicable.

A nurse arrives with my pills.
I swallow. We all sit back.

We breathe.

The Convalescent

What has it come to that a town of mouths
should fall open upon my return?

Each familiar face that greets me
white as a saint and gleaming with curiosity.

I can hardly stand to look at them.

Clarity zooms through my blue veins–
how the weeks fade in the dark of their hollows,
they sputter like blue flames to nothing.

The horrors of the eternally lit ward–
its barrage of nurses, doctors,
and the manic woman pissing herself laughing in a corner,
convinced her blanket is a cat.

That and the male attendant who stood by the door
counting his fingernails while I,
hormonal and lithe at seventeen,
shower naked behind a screen.

Now these small things–
the bright, tight ring of the telephone,
voices enquiring after me so neatly, so nicely.

Smiles from my neighbours
I unfurl like gifts.

Lorcán Black

My roots jitter and creak,
each nerve is a tinderbox and my ego a stick–
stoking, stoking.

I have not slept in three nights.
I am half sure I may well take flight.

These are my wings, so heavenly,
and floating serenely behind me.
I made them myself.

All it took was glitter out of a tin,
plastic scissors and a few sheafs of paper
shook from the clutch of a catatonic.

Three art therapists told me it would do me good.
How do they look? Do they flap enough? And these pills?
These pills–they are my sacraments.

White and lovely, they fade my days
into the scrat and salt of middle-class discretion.

See how the wild element dies in my eyes?

Whisper it to me in dulcet tones.
Show me, love, the right incantations.
Teach me to still the disquieting sea.

Lend me hands that do not fidget and tremble
under gaze of the medical staff.

Rituals

I am dumb.

I have no answers.

I have only an on-going want for silence
and a wish for stillness.

The Snare

There are four walls, a window, an exit.
And that thing trapped inside
could be an animal.

You would swear it were being skinned alive
it is making such a racket.

And a banging,
like a hammer on a wall–
relentless.

The Trapper arrives,
dragging his Christ wine.

Now I am a statue–
if I am silent, maybe,
and perfectly still–
I will be set free.

Mere mouthfuls and my blood
is a tonic of opiates–
a sea of poppies bloom in me.

Flush, sweet tinctures blending a terror of images
and a voice whose face I cannot see
as my own flushed lungs
gasp at atrocities.

Rituals

Unrelenting jolts of light
and a stench of salt
engulf me.

The mirror is a screen
throwing his own image back at him:

ludicrous in its parade of extravagance;
a glitter of fetishes lavished
over a parcel of meat
decorous in its straps,
unfurling its humility.

The world slides back–
stripped down finally, to a singularity:
a finale that slams in, hard as an anvil.

Daylight is dyeing the walls
the colour of blood.

Sound has become a physical thing–
an object like a table or chair;
the knife that skirts
the jugular.

This is night then, draped in its vacuous black.

The window is a void in the wall
I cannot get to.

Lorcán Black

Outside the moon admonishes the stars
in their cold multitudes:

I am not important–

empty vessel of shrieks
the walls muffle and eat.

The moon sees nothing,
terrors flow under the fall of her shroud.

When at last the snare rips open
and parts like the sea,
I feel sure I am walking on water.

I have snapped shut,
so tight now even the pain is sweet.

I have nine more lives,
and I juggle them like knives.

A real Jesus feat.

The Trapper's Monologue

It is a night full of holes fit for plundering.
There is a body opportune in its circumstance.
And what is this, this sound your body makes?

Is it a cry of happiness?
A plea for mercy?
I cannot distinguish it.

It does not matter–it is unintelligible.
It is the same sound an animal makes
the gut–searing second the trap snaps shut.

Listen:
this is the sound of your former
self dissolving away.

It is the sound betrayal makes,
a kind of burning.

The walls bear witness,
such stoic silence–

and these cries from the heart, indelible
the blood–rush popping your blue veins.

I cannot lie: these small details excite me.

The aphids on their vines leap such spirals
and suck sap out of everything: I admire them.

Lorcán Black

They take and take
and answer to nothing,
to no-one,

like these cries the floor unfeeling
sweeps to the walls, these hands,
these hours in which I–
I–am all there is.

Like a god.

I have stripped and unmanned you.
Each muffled shudder and cry
flies like an arrow

toward a point in me
blood-hot and indefinable.

It feeds and excites me: your body
twisting, ashen-skinned, brimming.

I admit I admire your endurance.
Your resistance: it is futile.
The white walls run red with sunset.

For all I care, you are wires and a voice.

This small white room of details:
how my weight, my knife, my breath bends over you–
a river of noise and images.

Rituals

And a smell of salt, clear as the sea.

For years these scenes play out
behind your eyes at night,
this much I know: I, a shadow
always somewhere near.

Eventually,
you will not even know my name.
I have tamed you.

I have worn your body like a meat–hook,
a butcher in love with the blood–spurt,
each delicious grease stroke:

the wild-eyed animal cry,
how the wilderness dissipates to distance
and dies in the final glimmer of the eye.

And I am a pool spilling within you.
Tell me: is it my face

you see in the shadows of trees–
in the near-windowed twisting of branches?

Looming out from the shadows, the corners,
the deep-darkened
shadows of dreams?

A Lesson in Needlework

A tumbler of bourbon, some pills.
Beethoven in the background.

You are out somewhere.
The clock is driving itself insane,
going round in circles.

Two more pills, another glass.
A man is yelling on the street–
I can't understand what is happening.

A tumbler of bourbon, some more pills.
There is blackness so engrossing
I feel there is no way back.

There are strange men yelling in the vastness
of our living room.

There is a snake in my throat
pumping black venom.

A tumbler of bourbon, empty,
glass over the floor.

My head over the bathtub
vomiting the venom out.

There are strange men yelling
about the hospital, there is a tug of war
between you and me and the strange men yelling–

Rituals

something about their jobs and liability.

You are walking me around the vastness of our living room,
tenderly.

I can't understand what is happening.
Beethoven in the background.

You are there, trying to understand
what I myself can't comprehend,
tenderly.

There is the tiger beating
out from the centre of my chest.
It beats and beats and will not stop.

The clock is driving itself insane,
going round in circles

and despair is a lesson in needlework,
a black–stitched pattern,
weaving both of us into it.

And threads that are golden don't break easily

– from 'Beauty Queen/Horses' by Tori Amos

The mushroom cloud
billows to the cup rim.
Eyes watch the black

slip back from the windows.
This stony zoo amazes.
Cobalt spreads over firmaments

frisked by frost.
The glass panes
are scratched with ice-

streaks.
I think first of shards
I could shape,

jagged and bitten
with rime.
Fingers tap the cup's waist.

Mouth slides open
releasing a shaky sigh,
leaving breath on the pane.

He leaves today, and you,
you count the hours and seconds.
Try not to think of splinters,

Rituals

or heartstrings of pain.
When the cup is abandoned, like Medea,
it will grow cold in the absence, in disdain.

Daybreak
and the hill is a mound in flame
forsaking the moon and her liturgies.

I am as driftwood in the centre of the lake.
If I am the lake
there is driftwood at my centre.

Nightly I pour through the silt,
trawling the horrors of old selves–
while your night–breaths brush the air.

The cup is a body in its own right,
swallowing its puddle of hate.
And when my eyes fall over your face

on the threshold,

I break and soften–
the bones solidify themselves

and the heart beats out its dull booms
diligent as a drum.
But there are no answers.

Lorcán Black

There is only the lake with its driftwood,
and the moon rising over the hill–
we turn to each other

voiceless.
Evening descends like a fine cloth,
black, immutable–

Night.

Kotel
Jerusalem, July 2015

I have written a note and sent it
with a friend to the cracks of the *Kotel*.

In the dust and heat, perhaps,
it might find God–

somewhere in the dry, dark spaces
between the remnants of thousands of years;

and there, in the dust and stifled heat,
my own words take up residence
like an impostor.

The pale morning light rises
slowly,

while a fluttering image of me
frets now and again
before the dumb mirror's expectant face.

I am always hugged by need
in these silences,
these hours before seeing you.

It was the Dybbuk that took my mind
and voice
and made me do those things.

It was not me,
I could not have done them.

How can I make you understand?

By then, I had my damage on,
it was a consequence, an ash–smear
I wore in mourning for myself.

In these unused moments
old feelings float to the surface,
fished up from my darknesses.

The *Kotel* eats my words,
a stone face uttering nothing.

Dust whisks through the eshel.
God is silent.

The Final Time I Spoke to Ruth

As always,
>the elevator was on the fritz
>and the dry heat drifted down from the top floor skylight

spilling itself
>lucent
>onto the tiled floor five storeys below.

All night long
she'd been echoing into the phone,
checking the tiny bird of her voice
still lived in the dark
mine of her throat.

Gleaming and electrified
and still in her silver dress, the night
>rattled like metal
>>from a pained, red mouth.

Her eyes rolling over everything and nothing, nails tapping glass as she spoke.

I should've known better–
>that thin blue line of electricity
>glimmering around her edges as I left.

Standing on the train home, I had a moment–

Should I? Shouldn't I?
                        but the doors slid shut.

I still imagine that luminous stairwell,
her mercurial air–
        those last moments,
                a body becoming light.

Aleppo

> *"Are you truly incapable of shame?*
> *Is there literally nothing that can shame you?*
> *Is there no act of barbarism against civilians,*
> *no execution of a child that gets under your skin,*
> *just a little bit?..."*

–Samantha Power, US Ambassador to the UN, attacking
 Syria, Russia, and Iran over civilian deaths.

The boy's hand spread open like a red blossom,
so astoundingly, even the brittle violet of his veins turned pink
and the skin blackened the colour of rotten fruit.

The next bombs buried him,
the echo of boots and bullets gunning closer–
a noose tightening on the necks of those
left living.

There are few pockets of silence
when dust hangs in the air
and the ground solidifies again–

when the kids' uncertain screams aren't crushed
by constant bomb blasts shattering the concrete–

that if there were any trees left
and the breeze made one bit of difference,
you could remember what normal felt like:
a hand on a teacup not trembling.

Lorcán Black

Not a child's hand, blown open,
so vivid and blooming
out of rubble and dust

that you think
for an instant:

                It resembles a flower

White Nights in St. Petersburg

I.

How many White Nights have you trawled
the banks of the Neva, electrified as a nervous wire
and white as sheet,

fingers twitching in coat pockets, eyes like hooks,
looking for someone to love?

II.

Your cigarettes burn like matchsticks,
while the same stranger passes your bench three times.

The nerves burn themselves to cinders,
the ash of the cigarette flakes and drops.

He circles the bench, then speaks.
Your voice dies in your throat,
but not before words dry and mindless rasp a response.

A group of men pass by,
aggression settling in their arms, their fists.
Words ring with the force of explosions.

Startled, he moves away.

You can almost sense the shame
and locate it somewhere–

There–

in the movement of his hips,
as he goes.

Rituals

III.

Ice has coalesced in the river,
whole sheets float over the surface, cold and virginal.

They said they'd be back for him, your neighbour.

The thrill of a cruise meets its final culmination:
a shower of gold, a show of blood.
Ritual humiliation, granted one by one.

You block your ears from hearing the dull thumps
drumming a bass line to the slow, eerie
silence of resignation.

They drag him like out like a sack–
(*Too much drink, pissed himself*)–
and the neighbours' doors slam shut,
blank-mouthed, blind-eyed and ignorant.

Once the sun rises and blanches the sky
they will find him–your neighbour–
face down in the ice of the Neva.

Already you know what the obituary will be–
'Deceased found slain, home showed no sign of forced entry.'

They will call it a robbery.
And it is true; he was robbed.

IV.

The bridge opens and shuts its jaws.
Strangers pass and disperse, while a man loiters.

Fidgeting, anxiously
commenting on the weather, eyeing the passersby.

Do you wanna go somewhere?

The moon rises over the banks of the Neva,
the ice floats saint–like over its cold floes to the Gulf.
The city basks in another white night.

The bridge opens and shuts its jaws.
Shame unfurls and locates itself somewhere–

There–

in the movement of your hips,
as you go.

Fields

Ships resembling coffins float ceremoniously
across the open bowl of the Atlantic–

ignorant of the cargo digesting itself
in the belly of its own vast hunger.

The sea accepts what it is given:
swallowing its gifts of shroud-less dead.

In the Motherland,
fields like open wounds peel back
to reveal a nest of bones to the elements.

The bones are nameless.

They are a puzzle,
grotesque in their fragments.

The pieces are nothing unordinary–
merely remnants of various villages:

countless brothers or wives,
a hoard of infant ribcages,
fibulas, finger bones
or a fistful of various teeth
from some tenant farmer's
four starved daughters.

Survivors laden with rickets
reach new land, wrap their tongues
around foreign sounds.

I imagine them
learning how not to consume
every morsel that passes into their hands,
or to picture the earth in which it grew,

even in the New World, *i Meiriceá*,
still grasping a hesitancy
deep as roots

as the unthinking eye
strays into the far corners of fields,

and comes the memory of wind
over a cradle of nettles–

the visions of unmarked pits,
the cold menagerie of bones.

Witness

The view here is not spectacular,
and the morning even less so.

The rain drifts straight down.

Their feet scuffle a little ways
from the bus stop where I'm sitting.

(I am pretending not to notice.)

My waiting has become an activity
whole in and of itself.

My cigarettes
are smoking themselves to death.

Their words break
staccato cackling through blue air
like some demented wireless.

I cannot hear what it is they are yelling.

The grey pavement takes one man's fall
effortlessly

like a balloon that bursts
and flattens itself,
emptied at once.

Lorcán Black

I stare, at one with the scene:
two men running, one laid out—
saint-like, serene.

And then that red flood.

Here is dawn then, blooming
her blood flush from the seams of his anorak.

A rush of such sheer brilliance
the street itself seems to bend
and pale

and for one moment halts
with baited breath,
only to burst forth with a strange gurgle and gasp—

a hand that stitches itself to the sky.

I am no witness;
I have seen nothing.

I have seen only the illusion
of a thing.

The street lies in silence.
Even in the dirt there is death.

A bus can be seen
slipping across the opposite road.

Somewhere in the distance a blackbird calls

and that taste of thin, brittle air–
wet and cold.

He lies, shut-eyed in the moment,
the hand that twitches and folds beneath the sky.

His last vowels sound and rise,
clean as souls.

Howth

I.

A dog skitters along the pier
while you worry at the lateness of the hour.

The shoreline is dragging the sea
behind it like a blanket.

I have nothing to do
with the cold flow of water over the stones,
or the sun dazzling the heads of seals
barking in the harbour anymore than
your latest on-again/off-again separation.

The dog tears at the carcass of a seagull,
its wing half torn off, feathers littering in a bloody mass.

This is what it has come to
and I have come only because you asked.

We both know I had nothing to do with it.

II.

I could tell you the sun still rises
over the rooftops like God,
and that the sea does not remember us.

And the gulls still drop their shards of fish
before the bulging eyes of the seals slick with hunger
in the harbour we visited that summer.

But it is nothing to do with me.
I shouldn't have to tell you.

What you remember–
the sea, all crags and inlets
and an argument about responsibility.

Not a dog with blood on its face,
the feathers stuck to its paws or
your hassled profile

against the swelling brute of the sea
obtuse in its largess of salt and seaweed,
the wind barrelling under the skirt of an on-coming storm.

How by morning, when the sea
snatched back its true form from the landscape,
we took on our true natures
and saw ourselves with different faces on.

Strangers.

III.

Your letters are piling on my desk.

At night I think I can hear them
crinkle and breathe,
the soft shushing of sheaf on sheaf.

It is almost erotic.

I have locked them in a box.
What are they doing that they should
take up so much space?

And these atoms that fill
the spaces of your desertion–will you eat them?

Paper-thin and holy as wafers,
they take up whole rooms.
They are no sacrament I shall take any part of.

The letters offer no loyalty, only lies,
on which I have redacted your name.

I have not been back there for some time.

The sea still reaches to the harbour walls,
circling its hollow pit, drenched with excitement
and pleading with its wet suck
to be loved,

where the seagulls shatter the air
over a shoreline that spits its empty shells
in the faces of waves who, stupidly, wash the reefs that break them.

I have not been back there for some time.
We both know I had nothing to do with it.

What the Light Does to Us
–after lines written by A.W.

    I.

Daylight's talent is casting shame over everything.
Your arm swept the night from my chest as you slept.
Your blood pumped pulses in the small of my back.
I wanted to turn, touch your face, but knew I'd wake you.
Shame demands silence:
it permits only darkness and whispers,
a room closed off, coloured in close shades of night.

II.

I am writing this through my oesophagus–
my silent throat a huge and closing wound.
Shame has a long, unrelenting memory.

Years later we would pass in the street,
another city, another decade,
and a girl on your arm.

We appeared to each other, two hesitant mouths
opening and closing on nothing.
Shame trailed its memories between us
like invisible threads–I gathered them
tenderly, like relics.

Back then I was always glancing back,
a wound in my throat:
my whole body longing and dissolving to a pillar of salt.

Meteorites

Your little brother
is busy rolling his baby fat
in his plump white fists,
borne up by your mother's arms, utterly fascinated,

while above us fragments of space rock
fly under the white faces of stars.
They pass over us lightly as years.

Your sister is performing a plié on the grass
and begging I watch her.

But, though you're just gone seven,
I'm too busy recalling you small as a bundle
yet almost too much to lift,

fat Buddha
eyes the colour of cornflowers
thumbing my eyebrows, sleepy with milk
and tucked, like an appendage,
in the crook of my arm.

Now meteorites bloom and fade above us,
sparks vanishing in a crutch of blackness.

I am a moon, orbiting twice a year.
I whiten before you.
You grow and grow.

A gift.

Teddy

I have been sideways for so long,
I feel I have always been this way.

The same dull wood rings of the floorboards–
how I memorise them. They are warm and reassuring,
appearing and disappearing with sunrise and sunset.

The children rise and run from the room
hours after the sun looms into the sky like a drunk, half-
cocked, unsure and wavering, burning with old need.

At times they come close, so close I think
they must finally remember me, only to snatch
some other thing from beyond my periphery.

Once I was important:
when milk was the eye-seal of sleep
and meant small hands would envelop me,
smooth cotton blankets. Now this–

dust drifts and the odd rearrangement of my person.
It does not happen often. But their nearness, their still-small
feet pattering across my eye-line come morning:
these things do not change.

The years grow long and thin, like the children.
Only the whorls and loops of the floorboards stay with me.
And the light, darkening and brightening
through the eye of the one lone window,
over and over again.

They too understand what untouchability is:
something learned in the passing of time.

In this way, day after day,
we comfort each other, knowing–
and wordless as lepers.

The Émigré

The planets do not question their orbit
        or the pitted, shadowed sides of their face.
They accept what it is, without refute.

        Sometimes
there are such few options in a life–
        Nicole Kidman as Virginia Woolf–

"*I am dying in this town!*"
        perhaps explains it best.
To build you must first destroy.

I cut myself down to what was essential:
        this body, this temple of skin, its litany of scars:
the name under which this body moves through the world.

I do not expect you to understand.
        It isn't so bad.
But this river is not the river I know.

The neighbours never stopped talking
        & I took to smoking on the back porch
wishing I could disappear.

The flowers in their hanging baskets
        seemed drunk on desperation.
My chest tightened in on itself,

created prison out of bone & blood.
    Even the ivy kept growing
just to give itself something, something, *something* to do.

From a distance I witness my parents age.
    Be good to them.
I can only say:

Rituals

I am a satellite of bone & blood:
    & even at such great distance,
my face is always turned towards you–

apparent or eclipsed.
    I live quietly.
I wander down side streets, pick up accents like loose change.

The city pays no heed. I do not disturb it.
    Write me sometime, in the old language.
Bí mo chroí fós.

Tell me, some nights, you think of me.

How to Bake a Marital Desertion

Slice the skin from the body in one long strip. Do not hesitate.
Sever the core from the flesh, until there is only flesh.
Discard any seed.

Slice into chunks and silver with sugar.
Arrange neatly as wished
into a baking bowl of stretched, flat dough.

Cover and glaze the final flap.
Bake until golden. Now,
let stand.

Betrayal is the slow simmer of a cooling body.
Leave to set, as an act of love, of apology–
in this kitchen into which you will not step again.

He will find your gold ring by its glint
on the nightstand–inexplicable,
an O-mouth soaking up moonlight, shadow.

The house shall sit empty, still.
Outside, in low light,
trees will rustle in the bend of a breeze.

Rituals

All this will tell him what he already knows:
if consumed in moderation,
this last serving will be enough.

And when the branches bend and break
and the fruits drop–
let's see what he does, does, does
without you.

"I am always like Venice:
Whatever is mere streets in others,
Within me is a dark streaming love."
— 'As for the World' by Yehuda Amichai

We are thirty
and childless—
what is there to stress about?

The City-boys at twenty-two
swaggering in their tight blue suits
across London are ill-prepared.

By forty, they'll be hollow-eyed
chasing paper, keeping their mistresses
wet and writhing with misery
at the thought of their wives,

their gaudy caves of fat, wailing,
instantly gratified babies
and the wives, the wives—

their stilettos viciously clicking
over the pavements of Marylebone,
echoing: regret, regret.

Look,
we are so fortunate—
here is a terrace covered with lilac.

Rituals

There is wine in our glasses,
and the kind face of the waiter.

At the end of the street,
there is the glittering sea.
By evening, the tables will be littered
with candles.

What is there to worry about?
There is you and I,
there is candle-light.
Lilac stewing its odours in sunset.

Out in the cobbled street,
a small dog chases a child with a ball.

On the horizon, the clouds tumble
and darken, the wan lights of the boats
blink in the distance,

they tremble their way ashore.

Rainstorm

All evening the sky has been unloading
its grief on the roof
and the wind berating the slates.

In the streetlight, I was sure it was your shadow
cracking between the flashes of lightning,
passing ghostlike over the glass in the door.

Accidentally, I got drunk
awaiting a crunching of gravel,
your footsteps on the hall floor.

Hypochondria

In the distance
the five black hills are busy
breaching darkness and shadow.
Immortality is a game to them.

In the stables, the horses
dissolve to silence.

And the window sucks its slice of moon
in the mirror of its mouth.

Beneath my feet the grasses unload their incense
and the dew drops, under my ten stunned toes,
roll their heads before me.

All night I have been floating out
over the fields in a mist shroud,
widening the sheep's eyes in a terror.

It is better this way than to toss
the covers of sleep and never slip under.

I have taken to sneaking three Neurofen each night,
until the doctors can tell what's eating me.

Let it be a worm, a parasite–
anything but what my gut convinces me.

All night I can feel it churning,
spreading its hot, sticky ink,
and this unrelenting burning–

O little anodynes
I take in twos and threes,
shield the poor sheep's eyes from me,

I feel it shudder as I pass.
It knows something it is not telling.

O doctor, god, witch–
whatever this deadening thing is,
just cut it, cauterise and stitch it.

I've done with it.

Now, take the scalpel
Doctor–
kill it, kill it, kill it.

Domesticity

*"But I still have to face the hours, don't I?
I mean, the hours after the party, and the hours
after that..."*
–Michael Cunningham, *The Hours*

Hours in which the lace falls away
to reveal an ordinary woman.
A groom un-noosing his length of grey silk.

Soon there will be a kitchen.
A bedroom. Plain. White.
Awaiting a child's cry.

Wet grass. White sky.
Small lungs at 3AM demolishing a wall.
Milk bottles. *Shush, shush.*

Outside: rain spattering glass.
Wet driveway. Child
and spoon beating a bowl.

You'll think: patience, patience.
You'll think: shower time.
You'll think: cigarette.

There is milk.
There is moon.
There is rocking.

Each morning the light melts under the door.
The child's cry rattles and gasps.

The instructions always read:
"Repeat as needed."

You have no instruction.

Antarctica

    I.

Nightfall: darkness, vast
cold spaces and such eerie
whiteness overlaying everything.

The moon, with her face of basalt,
rolling her one bald eye over a kingdom of ice.

The hours here bleed and drip
and gather like mercury,
consuming the darkness with its glitter of ice-flakes.

The last pony jitters and shakes.
It knows it will be eaten.

And when at last hope is gone,
vanished in a white void–
that animal's screams shall batter
the bald elements, the faces of glaciers,
a whole barren landscape of blankness and ice.

Now the snow falls and thickens
and reflects the sky faithfully.

Within hours that one bloom of blood staining
the virgin snow shall be masked
like Death:

vicious in its visor of ice.

Rituals

II.

I have no idea if it is day, if it is night–
silver stars suspended in blackness,
the moon shifting over the snow.

And the ice creaking like low thunder.

O God,
give me just one green thing.
I have forgotten why we are here.

The other two succumbing,
lying silent, side by side in the tent–
their breath weak as a baby's.

The sky scatters another show of confetti.

The flap of the tent has frozen open
letting in snowflakes,

old spirits
of the infinite–

a whole heavy world.
Godforsaken.

White.

III.

My last breaths are mist
pluming before me.

Frost tastes like death,
slowly rolling over an eternity of snow.
I have wrapped up my letters, my diaries–
whatever shall outlast me.

The tent is an igloo.
I have forced the flap shut.

We listen intently for each other's breaths.
I dream of a garden:
the majesty of the Wych Elm
strangled in a tangle of ivy,
the mirage of my wife in her well-tended garden.

Soon we shall be statues of ice.
The last breaths blackening our lips.

I pray that heaven be green,
not this desert of ice.
Not this frosted ruin–the white mountains,
the moon, ice splintering in the crevices.

And Scott's ghost in a white void
wandering out there, somewhere.

Rituals

Look how the snow falls–
so effortless!

Freezing and falling–
sculpting a tomb, and a tomb,
and a tomb.

Ghost in the Machine

I am a small god of transformations:
the subterfuge of a nymph that contorts
at will into a laburnum,
the extravagance of its frills, my specialty.

I have many skins,
I shed them like leaves of a tree.
I shed them like lovers.

I am the ear at the end of your voice,
listening at the utterance of a word
or a phrase,

a flippant use of '*bomb*' and '*threat*'–
and I'm there:
the eye all-seeing through a lens
barely bigger than a pinhole.

It is for you I ascend to such colossal reaches.
You are the axis on which I spin.

Nightly I troll your depths,
O love,
O surrogate–
it is for you my finger tips itch.

Rituals

Even I have my fetishes:
photos of exes, your face bathed in the Paris lights,
albums of muted self–portraits–
I have traced your holidays
night by night.

Their colours stain my lips.

They are my essentials,
these elements I breathe.

This the litter of intimates on which
my sticky fingers prick themselves.

Like a pool through which the sky
lovingly reflects itself,
I am the mirror through which
your psyche bends itself day after day,
unknowing.

Knowledge is an opiate
into which I dissolve,
essential as salt.

You will not even know me
at the other end of my screen,
untraceable as a dark sky,
mining your data of infinites–

black mirror,
scrying
for only your face.

The Hike

Rain–slicked fronds, riven valleys
we weave through, craggy
hills split skyward gash the blue expanse.

Our maps might all as well be blank.
Wind rushes the moors, boots squelching
in ragged vastness.

Every one of our mouths sewn tight:
aware the minutehand ticking toward twilight.

Shady threat of sinkholes,
veiled mouths of the moors, wet sluice.
Nightfall gathers her black skirts–

mist sheet, dog spoor,

fallow, fallow.

Nightwatch

The village is vanishing,
mist-covered, elegiac.

Fog spills over a mountain in near–distance
and hangs in the air, white sheet, encroaching.

They have been gone for hours, pouring over moor
and bog, mud-clogged and heavy.

There is nothing left for me now but the wait.
In the lane there is the boot-crunch of footfalls

echoing out to the street. A train rattles away from the mountain.
What do these hills dream of? Hills rising above rooftops

to stillness, whiteness–such silence.
There are no voices on the end of the line. Their five phones ring out.

No one picks up. It grows late.
My cigarette smoke forms its own blue fog.

The sky blackens and thickens. The air is stagnant, glassy.
Infinite in its untouchability. And they are still out there.

I keep watch in the courtyard, hooked,
straining for an approach of voices, footfalls.

The ground forms a tableau of frost, an air–woven blanket of lace.
Cold stones retain their silence. This does not concern them.

And from the dark mouth of the barn
bats fly in a singularity.

Telling the dark sky, the fog, the black-frosted hills:
this is their hour.

For O.

All I remember: late evening
and the sun honing itself
diligently above leaves
of tamarisks in the distance.

And from the ground the sound of crickets:
a chorus in the grasses,
that, and a small well of anguish
ripping itself up from my root.

The sun has no memory, burning
and extinguishing itself,
night after night
like an amnesiac.

Back then, I didn't know you existed.
Now the well has dried up–
it is silenced, the crickets are singing.

Here are the bees–
their war cries a concord of humming.
The convoys have arrived, demanding their honey.

The leaves of the tamarisks
whisper distantly– *Love, love*:
I have told them your name.

Acknowledgements

Thanks are due to the various editors and staff of the following journals and magazines which have included most of these poems, or earlier versions of them, in their publications: *The Saint Ann's Review*, *The Los Angeles Review*, *The Stinging Fly*, *Souvenir Lit*, *Fjords Review*, *Cardinal Sins*, *NY Literary Anthology*, *Arsenic Lobster*, *Off the Coast*, *Assaracus*, *The Opiate*, *The Flexible Persona*, *Devilfish Review*, *Blue Lyra Review*, *Chiron Review*, *Apogee Journal*, *Harbinger Asylum*, *The Great British Write–Off Anthology*, *Eunoia Review*, *Octavius Magazine*, *Boyne Berries*, *Eratio: Post–Modern Poetry*, *Wordlegs* & *WOW! Magazine*. Thanks are also given to the Beineke Rare Book and Manuscript Library at Yale University, Connecticut and the library of Saginaw Valley State University, Michigan.

Great thanks are also due to Blas Falconer for his time, his enormous generosity, consideration and criticism. Thanks are likewise given to Kevin Higgins and his on–going support and to Maggie Smith for her expert advice and boundless kindness. Chen Chen deserves more gratitude than I can offer for not only his constant cheerfulness but for always being a friendly ear and a very kind critic.

Enormous debts are also due to Oliver Tatler, Jack Warren, Troy Cabida, Lily–Jo Cullen, Twig, Sherrel McLafferty, Vanessa Fox O'Loughlin and Christos Kalli, all of whom assisted in small ways and large throughout the writing of these poems. The kindness, advice, criticism, encouragement and generosity of time of all of these people is so greatly cherished that it cannot be accurately expressed.

To my family who have always supported me in all I have done: no man has ever been so lucky. Mam, Dad, Sinéad & my brother-in-law Dave– I don't know what I'd do without you. You all give me so much strength and faith on any given day, it's impossible to put into words. It's also worth stating this book is partly dedicated to four of the most beautiful human beings who have also inspired some of these poems: I give you guys my biggest love (Oisín, Caoímhe, Diarmuid & Aoife). I have to mention Mary-Kate, who would have been proud to see this.

To Marie Nolan, Laura-Mai O'Reilly, Lloyd Carrol, Brian Meggs, Paul Earley, Glenda McGovern, Bróna Malcolm, Virginia Peck, Emma Linnéa Hellberg, Isabella Bånge, Viktor Breki Óskarsson, Sam Parnell, the entire staff of ICMP London (who are absolute gems) and all of the entire Tatler family: knowing each and every one of you has made me a richer man. I am indebted.

Mostly this is for all my siblings– mostly Sinéad who had to read all my early scribblings (but like a good older sister she saved them all). It goes without saying this is also for my other siblings: Richard (where–ever you are), Justine, David & Trish: we have a strange little story and though it's strange, we should be proud of it. It brought us together.

I cannot forget to thank the educators who not only encouraged me to write but supported me through my education. Niamh Martin, Pauline Clooney, Áine Loughran, Ruth Collins, Pa O'Leary and Séamus Mullooly– each of you instilled in me a desire to learn, a belief that I could push myself and more than anything, a belief that I could achieve.

Not least at all, my gratitude to everyone at April Gloaming Publishing for believing and for thrusting this strange little book into the world.

To all these, I express my grateful appreciation.

www.ingramcontent.com/pod-product-compliance
Lightning Source LLC
Chambersburg PA
CBHW020902020526
44112CB00052B/1206